CON'. VEGETABLE GARDENING:

Discover the secrets for growing fruit and flowers in a container even if you are a beginner.

Plant vegetables and herbs in your backyard all year round

THOMAS URBAN

Table of Contents

Introduction 1

What to Grow In Container Gardening 6

Basics of Container Gardening and Its Advantages 20

Planning What to Grow And When 28

Types of Soils To Use 40

Tips and Tricks on How to Build Your Vegetable
Garden 46

Detailed To-Do Lists in Vegetable Gardening 56

What Are the Mistakes That You Have To Avoid 62

Nurturing Vegetables and Plant Directory 66

How Do I Prepare For Winter and Provide Good
Growing Conditions 76

How to Choose Your Container 82

Tips for Container Plants 90

Managing Pests and Diseases 98

Conclusion 104

Introduction

Vegetable gardening in the city isn't what most people think of when the topic of growing your own vegetables comes up.

Contrary to common belief, you need not have acres of open land to grow a beautiful garden – whether this is of flowers or edibles. You can very well do it in containers. All you have to do is consider each container as a small plot private to each plant. With the help of containers you can build a most beautiful and useful garden within your home or outside.

In other words, container gardening is just a portable garden. This type of gardening comes minus the troubles of a regular garden (such as weeding and most pests), yet with all its benefits. Do not think or limit yourself with thinking that container gardening means indoor gardening – though this is mostly where it is used most. A container garden can be set up outdoors as well. In fact, most people who move a lot use this model so they can take their garden with them when it is time they move. Some of the most beautiful outdoor gardens can be container gardens.

The guide is specifically designed for container gardening and the unique needs plants have when they are being grown in containers instead of the more traditional route of an in-ground garden. While much of the information provided can be useful for any type of gardening, readers should know that from this point forward, all of the tips and techniques presented are understood to be meant especially for container gardening.

As to the label of "organic" gardening, organic refers to the methods used to germinate, grow, protect, and harvest vegetables without the use of any chemical products that are unhealthy for human consumption as well as the environment. Every now and then, any kind of gardener (even the experts) might be presented with a situation that requires chemical intervention to resolve, but chemicals are rarely the only option and should be considered as an exception to the rule – not normal routine. This guide seeks to provide alternative suggestions of healthy, biodegradable products and methods that can be used in place of chemical substances most of the time. One of the reasons why most people are interested in growing their own vegetables is to avoid the use of chemicals in their soil additives, plant fertilizers, and disease treatment and prevention because at least portions of the chemicals wind up in your food no matter how careful you are. All of the very necessary tasks involved with gardening can be done using natural products that are usually substantially less expensive than their counterparts are and significantly healthier!

Not all people are blessed with a lawn or a space in front of the house to test their green thumbs. People are clustered in apartments and in small houses. You can create your own garden, by planting in small containers. The container can be bottles, tubs, boxes, urns or barrels. The gardening in containers can be made better by grouping more than one plant, in one container.

If you are new to the gardening process, containers are very easy to handle. Placing the containers around your house will be easier than finding a soil path near your house. Even if you have a space in front of your house, you need to tend it and make it suitable for planting. This would take a lot of time and you would need to put in a lot of energy; there's no doubt about that. If you are an expert in gardening, the containers would help you to cultivate a lot of plants, in a very small area. You can use drop irrigation process, without causing yourself, many hassles. As your expertise grows, you would be able to choose the right plant and the right container.

The first reason is that people are eager to have a garden and the lack of space cannot stand as a valid excuse not to live in a clean and green environment. Container gardening is not a temporary solution. Many container plants can last for more than a couple of years. All it needs is commitment and efforts from your side. If a plant can grow in your environment, you will be able to grow all the vegetables, you require. If you have the right place and the right type of container, your plants will flourish.

No matter where you live, container gardening is possible. You can sustain your plants through extreme climates too. Rearranging the containers and creating different décor is possible. The most important reason for many people to take up container gardening is that it is one of the easiest ways to decorate a home, without putting the bank account, at stake.

Many people feel that container gardening is too difficult or too cumbersome to start and maintain. Nothing could further from truth. Anyone can start a container garden, even if you have no idea about gardening, containers, plants, etc. you can still start and set up a very beautiful – not to mention fruitful – container garden.

The container garden is one that you could move anywhere you want to go without any trouble. There is a lot to container gardening from selecting the containers and the plants to the ways of using them to decorate your house. All you need is a little commitment, a few dollars to spend and your valuable time.

What to Grow In Container Gardening

When you begin container gardening, you may want to begin with some of these easy vegetables and wait to branch out to the more difficult ones. After all, it's better to be successful the first year rather than be discouraged and end up not trying again the next year. Stick with these plants and you'll see results in no time!

Almost all types of vegetables adapt themselves well in containers, provided they get enough space there and required care is taken. Varieties of many large-sized vegetables specially bred to grow in pots or containers are available in market. So these days, the limitations on the part of selection of vegetables to grow in limited space are least. The list of such vegetables could be a long affair, but to start with most commonly consumed vegetables than grow well in containers are listed below.

Beets

Beets are actually really great container plants as long as you have them in a pot that's twelve inches deep. You can grow up to six regular sized beets in one pot, and even more of the smaller, baby variety in the same pot.

Beans

Bush beans work really great in pots. They should have a twelve-inch deep pot and you'll need to check the root growth to be sure they're not growing out of the pot. If they are, they have to be transplanted to a larger one. The other variety, pole beans, are going to need a trellis attached to their pot so they can grow up like they're naturally supposed to.

Carrots

One of the most 'easy to grow' vegetable and also commonly consumed one. They manage to live well in containers too. Since growing carrots is effortless process, a good choice for beginners. It may not save considerable amount of yours, but growing carrots at home ensures you of quality and healthy supply of vegetables.

If you're interested in growing carrots in a container pot, then you might want to start with these varieties.

- Short n Sweet
- Thumbelina
- Little Fingers

They're all baby carrot varieties that shouldn't get longer than four to five inches, but in case they do, have a pot that's at least twelve inches deep, if not more.

Cole Crop

These are broccoli, cauliflower, and cabbage, and they are some of the easiest vegetables to grow in a container garden. You should not plant a lot of types in a single pot because they won't be able to grow. Give each plant a pot for enough space.

Cucumber

If you want to grow cucumbers in containers, then you might want to try the Bush Pickle or Salad Bush varieties. The plants are going to come out of the edges of the pot and may need a little trellis to keep them upright, so be prepared for maintenance with cucumbers.

One of the most 'simple to grow' item in the list, cucumbers can grow well in containers. You can get large yield with minimum efforts. Though they grow well in pots, they do not grow well in winter. So wait until the end of winter season and then begin plantation.

Eggplant

Eggplants only need pots that are twelve inches wide by five inches deep, but they are going to need some staking to keep them upright.

Lettuce and Micro Greens

If you want to start really easy, then grow some lettuce and micro greens. The size of the pot doesn't really come into play with these. Just take a little fertile soil, some seeds, and keep the soil moist so that you get some homegrown salad greens!

To have lettuces on your catalog of container vegetables gardening is perhaps wise thing. Quality yield of it will turn out to be a profitable affair and you will be satisfied to get good return for your efforts (though you may not need to put more, because lettuces are really simple to grow at home). They love to be alone, so do not plant lettuces with full of other vegetables around. Give the attention it deserve, check that the soil is not wet, protect it from strong sun rays and again don't forget to keep adding moderate amount of slow-releasing fertilizers, preferably compost but don't over feed.

Melons

If you've ever heard of the dwarf melons like Bush Sugar Baby, then you've heard of a plant that seems to have been made specifically for container gardening. These are micro watermelon types that will need a little support when they begin to get fruit, or they could rip out of the pot.

Onions

Green onions are the best for growing in containers. All you need is a bag of sets, a pot around four to five inches deep, and some loose soil. You can grow onions until they are their regular size.

This one is largely consumed item across world. Again 'easy to grow' one, perhaps it could top the list of vegetables that can be grown effortlessly. Needs no special attention. Just sow the seeds of it and leave it on its fate, except adding some fertilizers and watering them regularly.

Peas

If you're planting the baby pea varieties, you can plant six plants in a twelve-inch deep pot. The baby pea varieties are:

- Maestro

- Green Arrow

- Sugar Bon Snap Pea

- English Peas

Peppers

The bigger the pot for peppers, the better because they require a lot of soil, you can grow any kind of pepper in pots.

Potatoes

Second in the rank of best-suited vegetable for container gardening. Again, for same reason that it is widely consumed item, potatoes make good choice. Do not plant it with tomatoes.. Potatoes need little large and deep containers.

It's really great to grow your own potatoes, and they're easy to grow in pots! You just need a twelve-inch pot for three to four potatoes. Keep giving it water so the plants produce and make sure the stems are covered fully with the soil. In a few months, you'll get some early potatoes. If you have patience, you'll have even larger ones!

Radishes

This could top the list of 'easy to grow' vegetables and need no special care to be taken. Good option to consider for rotational planting. This is recommended for newbie of container vegetable gardening.

Radishes are really easy and quick to grow, even with small containers. All you need to do is scatter a few seeds on top and keep the soil moist.

Squash

Use a five to seven-inch deep pot so that you can grow healthy squash plants. You can start with some of the following varieties.

☐ Papaya Pear

☐ Cornell Bush Delicata

☐ Table King

Tomatoes

The most cherished and widely grown fruit in the globe is none other than tomatoes. It is consumed virtually everywhere. Tomatoes are perhaps best vegetable to grow in containers since it is medium rooted vegetable and needs comparatively less care.

Having delicious, juicy tomatoes that come right from the vine is easy if you grow the following varieties.

☐ Tiny Tim

☐ Patio

☐ Window Box Roma

These can all be grown in five-inch deep containers.

If you want to try another variety, you're going to need a larger pot.

With all of these varieties, it's just a matter of following the growing instructions on the seed packet and keeping the soil moist but not water-logged. Once that's accomplished, the seeds will grow readily. Just remember to fertilize every two weeks to keep them from losing nutrients.

Now that you know how to grow the vegetables let's talk about the pests that can ruin your efforts, and how you can get rid of them before they do!

Green Beans

If given due attention, green beans also grow well in containers. They require more amounts of water and a good combination of food-based peat and vermiculite mixed well in good soil will perform better for green beans. You can get sizable yield that will save lot on account of your household budget for vegetables.

Turnips

Since turnips do not require sunlight all the time, it is a fine option to consider for indoor vegetable plantation or to be put in shady areas in garden. Some varieties of turnips are ripe within as soon as one month, so it should be considered for interim plantation.

Parsley

Being high on demand, parsley is the fine choice to have it in garden. This herb manages well in containers and you may find them planted in window boxes and pots when it comes to the container gardening. Little more care needs to be taken. No ordinary soil and addition of some fertile supplements can do the magic.

Basil

Slow germination, may take little less than a month. Basil shares many rules of gardening with parsley, including the climate they both need to grow well. Cold climate retards the growth of both parsley and basil, whereas heat works in the favor of these herbs.

Cabbage

Here the list comes to the fine selection for salad. Widely consumed and cherished vegetable across borders, cabbage is high nutrient requiring vegetable and needs little more care. Consider companion planting if you have cabbage on your list of vegetables for container gardening. It needs good bed, some slow-release fertilizers, and shady space to help it grow well.

Sweet Corn

Yet another most preferred item in container vegetable gardening, because the name itself denotes that it tastes too good. Nutritional item, so you should include it in your diet itinerary. Being a deep rooted vegetable, sweet corn need a deep container and since it grows high, it necessarily has to be out under the sky. It requires relatively low nutrients so a good option to post-harvest replacement of high nutrient demanding plants.

Hops

Hops keep growing until they are well fed. If you love homemade wine and wish to do it yourself, growing hops are just perfect choice to plant in containers. These growing hops value your hard work and return you the desired yield for longer times.

Zucchini

This one grows quite fast. Its big bushes add charms to the greenery of your garden and the further big fruits pay off your efforts to nourish the plant. Fish emulsion if added to the warm soil that zucchini needs, the results will be mind blowing. But don't mind to give external support to the growing fruits that become really big and weighty. Zucchini makes a good option to consider as interval planting between two long crop cycle vegetables.

Though the list is long, it is surely incomplete. Try to plant these vegetables on a rotation basis. Some of the mentioned above may not match your likes but you can always start with others. As listing 'what grow well in containers' is important, equally important task is to mention what does not grow well in containers.

The list of what can and what can't be grown in containers is never-ending. But your efforts can definitely give you tasty vegetables and fruits in return. If done with dedication, vegetable gardening will not only grow you food, it will grow a farmer within you.

Consider growing vegetables in container and you will never have to worry about not getting the freshest produce around. You can be sure that you are eating the right kind of healthy foods.

Basics of Container Gardening and Its Advantages

Container parks are among the quickest growing sections of horticulture, if not the staunch supporter of organic gardening. Containers could be produced where old-style gardens are not conceivable including room balconies, little courtyards, sundecks, patios, as well as areas having poor top soil.

Should you not have adequate space meant for a veggie garden, growing inside containers stands an immense solution. They are an ideal answer for persons in rental states, with restricted mobility or having constrained time to be interested in a large scenery.

Using planters and pots allows you towards having a movable garden, which can flower and produce all the time. All you need to do is keep plants outdoor during the hot summer days, and as soon as it goes cool, just bring the plants indoors. By defending plants from the icy weather, you will always ensure a garden-fresh supply of spinach, peppers, lettuce, tomatoes, and tastier kitchen garden supplies.

Container greens can likewise work in place of an ornate showpiece for your counters. But what type of box should you seed in? An overall rule is, the larger the vegetation, the larger the planter. The type of planter, however, is very much depending on you provided it empties well besides not getting too warm sitting under the sunlight all daytime.

There are sufficient and good selection, but deliberate on the common mistakes and strategize accordingly. For instance, ceramic appears great as well as drains fine, but inclines to parch out rapidly and needs frequent soaking. Old timber barrels hold water a lot better besides not heating up so much, but are frequently heavy as much as subject to decomposing.

Hence, you need to be creative and try anything ranging from discarded teapots to ancient plumbing fittings. Good planter plants consist of herbs, garlic, ivy, shallots, and leeks, which do not have long roots besides requiring very small room to breed.

Vegetable planting is a valuable project to do as the results of your hard work can transpire at your banquet table. You must, however, first choose if you wish to produce your veggies indoor or out-of-doors. Both approaches have advantages and disadvantages to it. You also will have to reflect on conditions like lighting as well as pest control.

Thus, you need to deliberate on your present situation to arise to an astute choice. On the other hand, soil preparation, in addition to maintenance, can remain much harder when cultivating outdoors. Over some period, nutrients inside the earth can come about diminished through repeated implanting. Fertilizing plus disease management become additionally challenging, too. Large areas that need to be pH adjusted or develop clay resources to be fragmented down could be worrying. Preparing a planter and preserving it stays not required when growing outdoors.

Although little is needed, maintaining manure levels could be complicated when tending indoors. It is easy to accrue too abundantly. A great deal of upkeep must occur when seeking to attain a balance in draining out excess liquid and saving needed dampness.

Soil within indoor weeding never adjusts itself such easily as compared to dirt outdoors. It stands worse for plant life when you provide it too ample moisture contrasted to once you let it dehydrate. When working outdoors, putting up a programmed watering scheme is relaxed and reasonable.

It could be tougher to organize this by indoor sowing. It stays possible, but it would probably charge a great amount and be disordered. It may not merit all the distress if you have excessively many planters. Lighting generally is not a concern with outside gardens provided they are arranged correctly.

You ought to easily remain to give your undergrowth with sunlight for five hours daily, depending upon the weather you reside in. Lighting provides extra challenge for inside gardening. If you cannot find a ledge that provides the good amount of sunlight, you might find yourself needing to transfer your foliage around the home all day through.

This, however, does make regulating the quantity of sunlight received a bit easier. If the sun becomes too warm, you could easily shut the blinds to avert burning. Automated arrangements have remained designed solely for this reason.

Therefore, put plants beside the openings to aid create a sort of conservatory effect and save you the anxiety and expense of constructing a real greenhouse. While illnesses and insects are created in equal situations, it stays simpler to handle within the house.

Detailed inspections and supplementary chemicals stay necessary to battle such matters when located outdoors. Fungus remains prone to develop because of condensation on the greenery on a cold evening. It is also comfortable for bugs to place their spawns undetected once outdoors.

Many of the devices available currently, whether biochemical or natural, have incredibly unpleasant smells and will not be appropriate for interior use. Almost every insecticide is similar as plant-based oils possess an added pungent scent and remains more costly than biological sprays.

Whether you choose to have your veggie gardening at home or outside will be subject to your exact situation as well as what would work best for you. Each technique has difficult situations, but it is certainly worthwhile when you will be relishing fresh besides healthy veggies in a short time.

Gardening in containers has several distinct advantages – especially in urban locations. In many senses it also shares much with gardening direct into the ground but the requirements of keeping plants healthy (and productive) mean that container gardening has some specific needs. We will look at the advantages and the important factors to take into consideration when establishing a container garden.

The Advantages of Urban Container Gardening

Modern cities have evolved over the last couple of hundreds of years and during that period the land on which they are built has been subjected to a wide range of uses. Cities constantly evolve and regulations relating to the urban environment do likewise.

Unfortunately, pollution and land use regulations were not, in the past, quite what they were today. The legacy that this has left for us is not always the healthiest one and, in particular, the soil beneath our city streets may contain significant traces of many contaminants, including dangerous heavy metals. The good news is that container gardening helps the urban gardener to side step this potentially dangerous form of pollution.

Water pollution is not as easy to avoid even when container gardening and although a great source of water for your containers is the public supply this is often chlorinated. Plants do not always react well to chlorinated water and many gardeners are concerned by the effect on productivity that this has. Rainwater provides a viable solution and plants will benefit from nutrients found naturally within it. The ambient temperature of rainwater, as it falls or from storage within the garden, is also better for the plants themselves. Additionally, although there will inevitably be pollutants in rainwater gathered from the atmosphere, pollutants are filtered out naturally by the soil. Generally, it is accepted that the air pollutants found in rainwater are diluted to a great degree and will pose no threat to health. When storing water on site it is important to ensure storage is in opaque containers and nets are placed over barrels or tanks to ensure mosquitoes and other insect life. Harvesting rainwater for gardening is also a recognized benefit for the environment in general, reducing the pressure on public wastewater operations, sewers and drains. The impact can be particularly important in urban environments prone to severe flooding.

Air pollution can be high in urban areas and the location of your garden may well mean that this can be a significant concern. Close to busy highways, or in very built up areas (rooftop gardens in particular), the levels of pollution in the air may be high. However, these pollutants will only be found on the plants themselves. For consumption, it's wise to ensure that produce is properly washed before cooking or eating. Air pollution affects most plants but in reality these pollutants can be washed away and, unlike commercially produced food, you stand a good chance of understanding what pollutants are in the atmosphere where you grow the food itself!

Container Grown Plants and Their Needs

Containers have a limited amount of space in them compared to a larger garden in which plants are grown directly in the soil. This limits the amount of water and nutrients available to the plants and means that container gardening can be far more labor intensive than other types of gardening. For the serious container gardener this calls for some hacks! These hacks have been around for many centuries and can be seen on both large and small scales throughout the years. The simplest way to reduce the time invested in maintaining moist, healthy containers is to create containers with a built-in reservoir.

Water Reservoir Containers

The basic principle for creating containers with a combined reservoir is simple. The container simply needs to be constructed with a false bottom and a tube connected to this.

The reservoir should take up between five and fifteen per cent of the depth of the container. An overflow should be drilled into the side of the container, at a level just below (or equal to) the false bottom. The false bottom can be constructed using a water permeable material or simply have several holes drilled into it. Natural evaporation and/or capillary action allows the water to rise into the soil/growing medium, keeping it moist continuously while not make it too damp.

Planning What to Grow And When

One of the nicest things about container gardening with vegetables is you can grow food all year long; however, there are certain guidelines you will want to follow. If you want to plant vegetables like broccoli, peas, and carrots, you will want to plant them in the spring or fall. However, if cucumbers, summer squash and tomatoes get you excited, then once the danger of frost is over, and then you can plant so many things.

Obviously, if you are like me, you enjoy planting a variety of vegetables. This means some will be planted in the spring, while others can be started in the fall. Because not everything is started at the same time, it is important to plan what you want to grow so you will know when to plant your vegetables.

Along with planting a variety of vegetables, as I have shared with you before, vegetables vary in their needs. Some need shallow soil while others need room for their roots to spread out.

Herein, you will be given some guidelines of when to plant certain vegetables and what they will need to thrive. This will help you to decide what you need to think about and purchase for a fruitful growing season.

In the chart below, I have tried to give you an overview of some of the most popular vegetables people like to grow. It gives the name of the vegetable, when to plant, when to harvest, and minimum depth of the container to allow healthy growth. Please note: In the column that says, "When to Plant," this means actually planting a young plant into the soil. If you decide to start your plants from seeds, you will need to begin that process several weeks earlier. Be sure to consult the seed's packaging.

Vegetable Planning Calendar

Spring

What to grow	When to plant	When to harvest
Arugula	Late spring	Late summer
Beans	Late spring	Late summer
Beets	Early spring	Early summer
Broccoli	Early spring	Late spring – Early summer
Cabbage	Late spring	Early fall
Carrots	Early spring	Early summer
Cauliflower	Late spring	Late summer – Late fall
Collard greens	Early spring	Early summer – Late summer
Corn	Late spring	Late summer – Early fall
Cucumber	Late spring	Late summer – Early fall
Garlic	Early spring	Late summer
Kale	Early spring	Late fall – Early winter
Lettuces	Late spring	Late summer
Mustard greens	Early spring	Early summer – Late summer
Onions (bulbs)	Early spring	Early fall
Peas	Early spring	Late summer
Potatoes	Early - Late spring	Late summer – Late fall
Radishes	Early spring	Late spring – Early summer
Shallots	Early spring	Late summer
Spinach	Early spring	Early summer – Early fall
Tomatoes	Late spring	Late summer – Early fall
Turnip greens	Early spring	Early summer – Late summer
Zucchini	Late spring	Early summer

Summer

What to grow	When to plant	When to harvest
Beets	Early summer	Early fall
Cabbage	Early summer	Late fall
Carrots	Early summer	Early fall
Corn	Early summer	Early fall
Eggplant	Early summer	Early summer – Late summer
Peas	Early summer	Early fall – Late fall
Peppers	Early summer	Late summer – Early fall
Squash	Early summer	Late summer – Early fall
Sweet potatoes	Early summer	Late fall
Tomatoes	Early summer	Early fall – Late fall
Zucchini	Early summer	Late summer

Fall

What to grow	When to plant	When to harvest
Arugula	Late summer – Early fall	Late fall
Broccoli	Early fall	Late fall – Early winter
Cauliflower	Early fall	Late fall – Early winter
Collard greens	Late summer – Early fall	Late fall – Early winter
Kale	Early fall	Early winter
Lettuces	Early fall	Early winter
Mustard greens	Early fall	Early winter
Radishes	Early fall	Late fall
Spinach	Early fall	Early winter – Late winter

If you notice from the chart, you can plant numerous vegetables both in the spring and in the fall. It makes it possible for you to enjoy some of your favorites throughout most of the year.

Here are some additional factors to consider when choosing the plants for your containers:

1. Determine which plants will fit in your available space.

2. Consider whether you will have to move your plants around or not. Large and heavy containers are much more difficult to handle than smaller ones.

3. Make sure your plants are suitable for the climate you live in. For instance, there are plants that need direct sunlight on a daily basis while others require indirect or filtered sunlight.

4. Think about choosing plants that have similar needs to each other. This means balancing watering needs with the size of the pot, the types of containers you use, soil types, and the size of vegetation you are growing.

5. Finally, think about your lifestyle. Your habits and routine as a gardener should allow you time to care for your plants. Do not take on more than you have time to handle.

Nothing beats the feeling of getting to use your own herbs and vegetables, and even flowers, straight from your own garden. There is a wide variety of plants that can be planted and grown in a container garden. With the right amount of planning, you can easily grow just about any type of plant you choose, given that their living conditions are met, of course.

- Plan which plants to grow. Plants have certain requirements that need to be met in order for them to grow properly. Therefore, you cannot just plant whichever plant you desire. You have to take into consideration the weather, climate and overall environment of where you live. Make a list of plants you want to grow and check their sun, water and soil requirements.

- Evaluate your house. Before you buy seeds or seedlings, carefully evaluate your house. Determine the areas which get the most sunlight, count how many hours the sunlight shines on those areas and identify the places which are partially shaded. Once you have listed those down, compare the requirements of the plants that you wish to grow and choose accordingly.

- Determine where to place the plants. If the area in your house which gets the most sun does not have enough space, choose to hang your containers or create shelves to place your plants on. This step is very important, especially if you plan to expand your indoor garden in the future. You can also choose to place your plants somewhere else and then move them outside to get some sunlight; however, the constant moving may stress them out, which can hinder their growth.

How to Choose your Plants

If you are an amateur at container gardening, then a trip to the nursery can be quite overwhelming for you. Plants are available in innumerable varieties and several different forms.

Considering the way plants are sold, transplants are the most popularly taken the option by people. These seedlings of vegetables and yearly blossoms are normally developed by vast wholesalers and sold at neighborhood garden centers in cell packs and modest pots. Despite the fact that transplants are the most looked-for plants when it comes to container gardening, there are several other varieties that can be used as well. These include seeds, bulbs, uncovered roots and several other forms.

You can think about a container arrangement as a house of living flower and foliage. For a long time of delight, ensure that the plant look engaging by ensuring that the roots are solid, and the foliage gains the light that it requires for making its own particular sustenance. Ideally, you must keep only one plant per container. However, plants that flourish in like soil, watering, and light conditions make fruitful blends.

Pick Plants with Similar Requirements

While making a choice of a plant, check the dampness, soil and light necessities of all the plants in the container. Distinctive plants adjust to the diverse situations of our planet. Plants that have adjusted to dry atmospheres have thick, waxy, or bristly leaves, which are capable of holding dampness. The foundations of these plants reduce the probability of their drying out between watering.

Equalizing the watering with the pot estimate, sort of container, soil sorts, and how expansive the plants are prone to develop in one season might require workmanship. It is fun and fascinating, and unlike individuals, plants might be traded, so don't be reluctant to analysis. In the event that plants fizzle, haul them out and swap them. Indeed, individuals with a "green thumb" experience a plant perishing occasionally. Just like the sweet-smelling and visual delights of plants and gain experience from your inescapable oversights.

Plant Shape and Texture

Winning container combos frequently utilize three sorts of plant shapes –

- Round, mounding plants - Fillers
- Tall plants - Thrillers
- Plant that hangs over the side - Spillers

Generally, these plant shapes fluctuate, in surface, estimate, shape, and shade, to make an unending blend of mixtures.

Leaf Size, Shape, Texture

You can put distinctive sizes, shapes and surfaces of leaves side by side. Differentiating size and surface are capable of giving an acting piece when finished well. On the other hand, rehashing comparative leaf sizes and surfaces might furnish a mitigating or concordant look.

Extent and Number

Whenever you are picking plants, think about a definitive tallness of the planting contrasted with the stature of the container. Outwardly, a satisfying extent is a one-third container to two-thirds plant tallness. As such, the plant material may be twice as tall as the noticeable part of the container. Alternately, when choosing the container, the parameter is switched - the container will be double the tallness of the plants.

Utilizing odd amounts of plants normally works well. With odd numbers, things on either side equalize to something in the center. Masterful cultivators regularly pick odd amounts of plants to achieve this symmetrical parity. Once in a while four blossoming plants look exceptional with a fifth foliage plant. Try different things with numerous blossoming plants and one intriguing foliage plant.

Shade Considerations

Picking a shade area will give your container arrangement a "pulled together" look. To pick a subject, think about:

- Colors supplementing the foundation where your container will be put

- Colors you have picked for interiors of your home
- Leaf shades of a specific plant you like
- Colors of nature from the district you live in
- Colors and styles that reflect a spot you want to visit or might want to re-make, for example the lakeshore, the tropics, or the north woods.
- Your most beloved shades

Contemplate a specific setting when choosing your plants and containers. The foundation could be different plants, porch clearing steps, wall, overhang rails, engineering siding, trim, or establishment materials. Shooting the foundation area of your container enclosure might bail you when selecting arranging containers and plants. Notwithstanding foundation, plants include an invigorating touch.

In the plant planet, your palette of unbiased shades grows to incorporate green, and tan, in addition to the regularly designated neutrals, for example light black, dark and white. These "neutrals" incorporate both plants and design materials. Off and on the foundation is the red block or having a blue siding.

Distinctive foundation shades influence how the same color looks. Case in point, light black, purples or greens look diverse against light black siding than they do against red block. They look distinctive still against tan limestone or white vinyl.

Color Wheel

A color wheel helps us to consider how shades function together. Take a look at the color wheel to perceive colors and their exchanges. Your living botanical plan will have a pulled together look provided that you pick one of the accompanying mainstream combos:

Monochromatic

- All one color tone like unadulterated blue, purple, red or yellow
- Tints (tint in addition to white), shades (tone in addition to dark)
- Monochromatic color plot has a tendency to be mitigating and classy.

Analogous

- Side by side colors from the shade wheel
- Analogous colors have a tendency to be agreeably quiet.

Complementary Colors

- Opposite one another on the color wheel
- Complementary colors have a tendency to make fervor and acting piece and regularly work best when utilized sparingly.

Color Wheel Families

- Warm colors incorporate orange, red, apricot, tangerine, terra cotta and yellow. Warm shades seem closer in separation outwardly.

- Cool colors incorporate blue, purple, fuchsia, orchid, maroon (and shades of pink). Cool shades increment the fantasy of separation. They work well when placed close to a yard or walkway, or a doorstep where they might be acknowledged up close. They have a tendency to mix with the foliage when seen from a separation.

- Neutral arrangement shades incorporate green, tan, tan, cream, white, grey hairs, dark. While green will regularly be recognized cool and tan warm, they assume such an extensive part in the scene that they frequently undertake the part of neutrals.

Lighting influences how your living botanical plan is observed and liked. Frequently individuals who work throughout the day take joy in white edged leaves and white or pastels blooms for their nighttime sway. The white "pops" during the evening. These same pale colors might seem washed out in shining light. Nonetheless, in the faint light of the morning or night, whites and pastels truly appear. Profound colors are lost in murkiness. When you are all over the place, perceive how light themes in the sun or shade influences.

Types of Soils To Use

When trying to start a container garden, it's important that you have good soil and good organic fertilizer to really start and keep your plants thriving. Soil will need to be every few weeks to every few months, depending on the plant. So choosing the right soil is very important. Garden soil is great, but it's not good when used by itself. No matter how great the brand looks, remember that it can't go into the containers on its own, not if you want your container garden to thrive.

Good Soil:

You need to choose a soil that is good for both aeration and drainage, otherwise you can't container garden. An artificial media, that has no real soil at all, is often actually best for container gardening. They're specially designed for this type. Some types that you can use are:

- Peat- made of partly decomposed vegetable manner, all of which would be organic to peat-land areas.

- Vermiculate- which is a mineral compound, and it's very moisture retentive.

- Bark- also a great way to stick with a natural option when trying to start a garden.

- Coir fiber- which is various coconut hulls that have been crushed together, a more natural option.

Usually you won't find these separately, but the artificial soil that you buy will have a mixture of all of them. For more options that are organic, it's important to stick to the organic materials.

You'll also find that different combinations work better for different plants. Make sure to research that works best with the variety of plants that you want to grow in your garden.

For example, if you're growing herbs you're going to want a soil that will retain less water than others. Something that contains more bark is better for these plants, and something even containing traces of sand is better than others are. However, if you're going to use a mixture that does not retain as much water it should be moistened all the way through once before going into the plot for planting.

Garden soil is able to be used, but only if you put something else in it as well. Peat moss is an acceptable substance to put with garden soil. It'll help it retain more moisture. Remember to never use play sand when mixing a sand type into your soil. It will kill your plants, and so will beach sand. Soilless media is much more costly than buying pure soil, so many people mix up to 25% of garden soil with their alternative to make it stretch further.

Making Organic Fertilizer & Compost

Organic Fertilizer:

Organic fertilizer is most likely going to do best for container gardening. It can also be inexpensive if you do it yourself. You can add many ingredients to whatever you have as well. Dried manure is the best way to have an organic fertilizer, and it's one of the cheaper options. You don't need cow manure for your plants to grow well because chicken manure is also a viable option.

Grass clippings can be added into the different pots and plants as well. It's a cheap way to add a little more nutrients into your plants. Grass will decompose quicker if you put it with a cup of water into a five-gallon bucket, it should only take one to two days before you can use this in your pots. You'll see a difference in the plants after only a week or two. They'll be growing healthier due to the rich nitrogen content. Make sure that when the grass has liquefied that you do not put the pure liquid into the plants, but instead you need to mix it with more water before placing it over your plants.

Seaweed is a little harder to get your hands on, but it is also a great way to add well need nutrients into plant soil, but you do have to wait for it to decompose. This can take longer than most people would like to wait. This is also best for outside plants due to the smell that decomposing seaweed and other substances may put out. Dried seaweed can also be used to make various organic fertilizers. You can also liquefy the seaweed as you would grass, and after diluting the liquefied form with water it is a great mixture for organic fertilizer. Seaweed serves as a source of food for soil microbes.

Coffee grounds are great to add in as a top soil to create organic fertilizer. The nitrogen in it will get down into the roots and give the plant a jolt. It's best for fruits like berries, but it also works on my flower plants as well. Just make sure to spread the coffee grounds over the soil before you water, and it'll filter deeper in as the plant is watered. You can do this with used coffee grounds as well, but fresh will pack more of a punch.

Human urine is also great for plants, and can be mixed into any fertilizer, homemade or otherwise. It's high in both phosphorus and potassium, which is great for your plants. You'll find these very ingredients in many of the fertilizers that are sold in stores. You need about one cup of urine for every eight cups of water, so make sure that you don't overuse the urine. If you put too much urine in the mixture, it can be detrimental to your plants, just like overwatering.

No matter what you use in your human fertilizer, you need to make sure that it's a mixture. You can add these together, but don't forget to dilute all the substances so that you don't over fertilize your plants. Container gardening is all about using what's right for the plants you're growing. Usually you'll be growing small to medium sized plants that don't require a lot of attention or fertilizer, so make sure that you're careful with the amounts you provide.

Compost:

If you'd like to get a barrel with a lid, or other container similar, it's easy to make your own compost as well. In the container you'd put various pieces of fruits and vegetables to decompose. The smaller the pieces that are put into the container means the faster the decomposition. This will produce a fertilizer that is both organic and packs a punch that will really make your container garden thrive and produce beautifully. It's best to use this type of fertilizer with fruits and vegetables to really add flavor.

It's also a great idea to mix in egg shells. Crushing the eggshells before you put them in will help them to decompose faster. The food will smell as it's rotting, so it's recommended that all composts are kept outside. When covered the smell will decrease but so will the rate of decomposition, egg shells actually are very high on calcium carbonate, which is the same thing found in lime, and it's great to fend off blossom end rot. It also makes your fruit grow better.

If you put potato ends into the compost you have to be careful that potatoes don't start growing in the soil. It'll eat up the nutrients from your composition, but you would have very healthy and ready to eat potatoes that are packed with flavor. This is the same for any root related plant.

However, the best thing to do for roses and most other flowers as well is banana peels. These decompose easily, and they'll keep your flowers very vibrant. Though they can also just be thrown in at the bottom of the dirt you use for planting, and then they'll decompose naturally without smell, but adding them into the mixture will help make your organic fertilizer that much better.

Tips and Tricks on How to Build Your Vegetable Garden

Now that we have talked about some of the basics of container gardening, Let's get started with giving tips on some of the things you will need. Below is a list of necessary tools you will need to guarantee your success:

Artificial lighting ~ Indoor container gardens will need light to allow plants and vegetables to grow, especially if they are located in an area without access to direct sunlight or an open window. There are kits you can buy that come with incandescent light bulbs, fluorescent lights and even high-intensity discharge lighting systems. Lighting is an absolute must for allowing seeds to sprout and for plants to grow indoors, even if you plan to transplant them later into an outdoor container.

Tools for Your Soil ~ there are several important tools you will need for your container garden:

- A hand trowel ~ the trowel is for helping you dig a hole in the soil so you can plant your seeds or seedlings. It can also be used to loosen old or hardened soil, and is helpful when adding new soil to your containers. You can also use a small handheld miniature rake and hoe to help you cultivate the soil around your plants and to remove weeds that may appear.

- Soil testers and moisture indicators ~ these make it easier for you to know when you need to water your plants. A moisture indicator helps you keep from over watering and to avoid not offering your plants enough water.

- A soil thermometer ~ This tool enables you to determine if your soil is the right temperature for your plants.

Tools for Watering Your Plants ~ You will need three essential watering tools.

- The hose-end bubbler ~ A hose-end bubbler is a tool that you screw onto the end of your garden hose that allows water to be dispensed through multiple holes. This allows for gentler watering of your plants so you do not create holes in your soil as the open end of your hose can do.

- A watering can ~ A watering can is one of the most basic watering tools you can have. Like the hose-end bubbler, it lets you water your plants without making deep holes in your soil and causing dirt to splatter. You can also use your watering can to mix up liquid fertilizer and distribute it to your plants gently.

- A spray bottle ~ For indoor plants, using a spray bottle to keep your plants well hydrated is a good option, too. Adjust the nozzle so it distributes the water or liquid fertilizer in a gentle mist.

Tools for Grooming Your Plants ~ An additional hand tool you will find extremely helpful is a set of handheld shears or hand pruners. These are used for clipping off dead flowers and old blooms. The hand pruners make it possible for you to clip stems and shoots that may be growing where you do not want them to grow.

When purchasing these hand tools, try to find stainless steel because of its longevity and make sure the handles are well made and strongly attached to the stainless steel, durable, and easy for your hands to handle and hold.

Planning Your Container Garden

Once you've decided the vegetables and growing medium for your container garden, it's highly important to sit down, plan and list all the necessary materials needed for the container garden. You should also come up with a step-by-step schedule in order to have a well-organized garden. This way, there is less room for error and you are able to save time, money and effort.

You should consider the location of your container garden, the types of containers you will need for your vegetable plants, the materials you will use such as watering cans, fertilizers, plant covers and other supplies that you might need to maintain your container garden.

Choosing the Location

When choosing the location for your container garden, you should consider the needs and characteristics of your vegetable plants. Some plants do well in shade while others need exposure to sunlight. Some plants grow well in cool temperature while others do best in warm temperature.

You should choose an area in your residence that has enough space for your container garden to grow. Vegetable plants, even though planted in separate containers, need breathing spaces for better growth in development. A crowded area is likely to result in plants with stunted height, short stems, small leaves, flowers and fruits. It should have enough space for you to move around.

You wouldn't want to accidentally bump on your vegetable containers or topple over a plant while watering or pruning the plants.

The location of your container garden should also have an easy access to water. You don't want to be hassled with the extra chore of fetching water from the kitchen or bathroom. Even though watering cans are readily available, it can be burdensome carrying water back and forth from one room to another, especially for people who have little time in their hands.

Choose an area with ample sunlight, shade or temperature most suitable to your plants. You don't want to constantly move your plants from one area to another for it to get the amount of sunlight or shade it needs. Some good examples would be windowsills, a porch, patio or balcony. These locations have good access to sunlight during the morning and enough shade for the late afternoon.

Consider the type of containers you're going to use for your vegetable plants. You wouldn't the extra problem of buying new containers because you found out that there's not enough space for your ceramic pots or wooden boxes on your patio or find out that there's not enough for hanging boxes in your window or porch.

Bear in mind the type of vegetable plant you're growing. Some plants will need stakes, poles or cages to grow and develop. Your chosen location should have enough space for both the container and the extra support structures.

Once you've chosen the location of your container garden, its time to consider the other needs of your garden.

Choosing Your Containers

There are different types of containers designed for different types of vegetable plants. Some are wide; others are deep while there are small and shallow ones. Containers also come in different shapes and color to add to the aesthetic value of your container garden. However, there are important points to consider when choosing containers for your garden.

Take into careful consideration the material used in making the containers. Some are made out of clay, wood, plastic or recycled materials. If the location of your garden is an area exposed to rain and the sun, avoid using containers made out of synthetic materials such as fibers and plastics. These containers tend to become brittle or deformed because of prolonged exposure to different elements. Also, avoid using dark colored containers. These containers tend to maintain higher temperature, which will ultimately harm the growth and development of your plants.

Choose a container with good drainage structures. That is, it drains water easily while holding enough moisture for the soil and the plant. Choose a container that is not too heavy and easy to transfer. There are times when you might consider relocating or rearranging your container garden and its best to use lightweight containers to make the task easier.

Use containers big and deep enough for the plants to develop and grow. Root or bulb vegetables need a deeper container for the roots to mature and develop, while others need a wide container to maximize plant growth. Below is a list of vegetables and the required container type and size:

Recommended Container Size and Type for Certain Vegetables

Vegetable	Container Type*	Size**	No. of Plants per Container
Beans	Regular (bush variety) With Support Structure (pole variety)	Medium-Large	2-3
Beets	Regular	Medium	Thinned to 2-3 inches apart
Broccoli	Regular	Large	1

Cabbage	Regular	Large	1
Carrots	Regular	Medium-Large (12 in. deep)	Thinned to 2-3 inches apart
Cauliflower	Regular	Large	1-2
Cucumber	Hanging basket With support structure	Large	2
Eggplant	Regular	Medium-Large	1
Lettuce	Regular	Small-Large	4-6
Onion	Regular	Medium-Large	Thinned to 1-2 inches apart
Parsley	Regular	Small	1
Pepper	Regular	Medium-Large	1

Radish	Regular	Medium-Large	Thinned 1-2 inches apart
Spinach	Regular	Small-Large	Thinned 3 inches apart
Squash	Regular	Large	1
Swiss Chard	Regular	Medium-Large	1
Tomato	Regular	Medium-Large	1

*Container Type: Regular (Wooden Box, Pots, Drums, Gallons, etc.), Hanging Basket, With Support Structure

**Size: Small (4"-6"), Medium (8"-12"), Large (>12")

Gardening Calendar

Once you've chosen the location and containers for your garden, it's time to create a planting calendar. A planting calendar is basically a schedule of chores and tasks in the duration of your gardening. It includes the gardening procedures such as seeding, transplanting and harvesting. Below is a sample planting calendar along with the basic description of the procedures.

Table 10. Recommended Planting Calendar for Container Gardening

No.	Task	Description
1	Crop Selection	Selecting the vegetables and varieties for the container garden
2	Growing Medium Selection	Selecting the growing medium to be used for the container garden
3	Location Selection	Selecting the location for the container garden
4	Container Selection	Selecting the container for the vegetables in the garden
5	Supply/Material Selection	Buying supplies and materials for the garden such

		as fertilizers, garden tools, insecticides and plant covers
6	Seeding/Transplanting	Planting of the vegetables either by seeding or transplanting an already germinated vegetable to your container garden
7	Maintenance	Regular caring for the plants by watering, fertilizing, composting or weeding
8	Harvesting	Harvesting the fruits, leaves and other edible parts of the vegetable

Detailed To-Do Lists in Vegetable Gardening

How to Utilize Crop Rotation in Raised Bed Garden

Vegetables, over most other kinds of plants, are vulnerable to Diseases and pests; left unattended, these nuisances multiply exponentially after recognized. Crop rotation is an effective way of combating a plethora of plant maladies.

Basics of Crop Rotation

The Idea of crop rotation trusts in the gardener's understanding of vegetable plant households and their associated insects and quirks. Rotation means not developing the exact same or a related harvest in precisely the exact same area in consecutive years, which will help decrease the buildup of illness germs and insects.

Sample Planting Plan

With some careful planning and Great record keeping, a Garden can have great harvest rotation with as many as four raised beds. In every succeeding year, plant crops from 1 bed in the subsequent one from the line.

Supplementing Raised Beds

In areas where lots of multiple beds are somewhat impractical, using big Containers to mature individual plants is 1 approach to enhance crop diversity whilst still keeping the integrity of a harvest rotation schedule.

Fertilizing and Keeping your crops Tomatoes are generally heavy-feeding plants. They like a soil full of organic matter and compost, but they also react well to side-dressing with fertilizers during the growing season.

Side-dressing -Side-dressing is incorporating a Little Bit of fertilizer around or even "on the side" of crops once they're growing. Side-dress using a complete organic fertilizer, for example 5-5-5, by sprinkling a little handful of those fertilizers around each plant., use the initial side-dressing when the tomatoes are golf-ball sized, and then use another side-dressing each 3 months then. Scratch the granular fertilizer to the top few inches of dirt. Use fertilizers with lesser levels of nitrogen; greater prices induce tomato plants to match a lot of leaves that are green and create few berries. Additionally, try not to find any fertilizer on the foliage; it may burn the leaves. If you would like to spray on your plants, treat your berries into some foliar feeding by mixing the fertilizer with water then spraying it on the plant leaves; this really can be a fast way to get nourishment into your plants. Employing fish emulsion or seaweed blend, dissolve the fertilizers in line with the recommendations on the bottle and spray on the plants every 3 months. Plants may take up nutrients quicker through their leaves than through their roots, but the effects do not last so long. Some research indicates that spraying plants with a seaweed mix may also decrease foliage diseases.

Tomatoes also enjoy Epsom salts. Studies have proven that 1 tablespoon of Epsom salts dissolved in 1 gallon of water and sprayed the transplant following planting and a month afterwards makes for healthier and more effective tomatoes.

Watering and mulching -Watering Is critical if you would like your berries to create the highest quality fruits. Generally, berries need 1 inch of water weekly, but they might need longer in areas with warm, dry, windy summers. Among the greatest things you can do in order to conserve moisture would be to mulch around your tomato plants. Plastic mulch can conserve moisture but is best utilized along with soaker hoses or even the ditch watering approach. The very best water-conservation mulch is really a 4- to 6-inch layer of hay or hay. The mulch is thick enough to stop weeds from germinating and prevent soils to dry off.

Straw mulches and hay keep soil cool, but berries love Warmth. Therefore, if you are in a Place that has cool summers, then wait till the soil has heated and the crops are flourishing before mulching with all these substances. Mulching and watering equally additionally prevent many fruit Issues, such as Blossom-end rust and fruit freezing.

Weather-Related Issues

Not all Issues With berries are linked to diseases or insects. Too much or too little fertilizer, too much water, chilly temperatures, and varietal differences can contribute to deformed fruits. Listed below are a couple of the common issues and some answers:

✓ Blossom Fall: Your berries are flowering superbly, but The blossoms all appear to fall without forming any fruit., this illness, known as blossom fall, results from air temperatures over 90 degrees Fahrenheit or below 55 degrees Fahrenheit. At these temperatures, most tomato blossoms won't place veggies. The remedy would be to develop varieties adapted to the warmth (like 'Solar Fire') or cold (like 'Cold Set'). Or you may shield the plants during flowering with floating row covers.

✓ Blossom-End Rot: During this illness, the underside, or blossom end, Of berries turns brownish and rots. Blossom-end rot is due to varying moisture conditions from the dirt, so the very best cure would be to mulch the plants nicely, plant them in well-drained dirt, and keep them .

✓ Fruit Cracking: several kinds of fruit cracking affect berries, but involve changing moisture conditions and vulnerability to cold temperatures early in this season. To avert this issue, plant varieties which are not as likely to decode (like 'Big Beef'), decrease nitrogen deposition, mulch the plants to maintain the soil moisture and shield flowering plants out of chilly nights with row covers.

- Sunscald: You will understand your berries have sunscald In the event the best surfaces of the fruit skins have gently colored stains. These spots, which are brought on by direct exposure to sunlight, eventually rust. To steer clear of sunscald, develop indeterminate types that have a great deal of foliage to color the fruits (like 'Better Boy'), prevent pruning the leaves, and supply afternoon shade with color fabrics. Or you may grow the plants instead of staking them.

Fertilizing and watering suggestions

Eggplants and Peppers are sensitive to excessive fertilizer, particularly nitrogen. Plants fertilized with too much nitrogen will develop big but have few veggies. But don't neglect pruning your crops; just avoid using high levels of nitrogen fertilizers. Rather, apply a two - to 3-inch layer of compost over the bed and also a tiny number of 5-5-5 organic compost around every transplant. Watering is especially important through 90-degree weather when water pressure and high temperatures may cause blossoms to fall. Side-dress (insert fertilizer around the plants throughout the growing period) around the drip line (where water obviously drips off the ends of leaves) of this plant using a tbsp of fertilizer, for example 5-5-5. To present your peppers a grow , combine 1 tablespoon of Epsom salts in 1 gallon of water and spray on the pepper plants whenever they are flowering.

Pest patrol

If you see holes at a pepper fruit and Locate a little, white pig within the fruit, think about it your introduction into the pepper maggot. The adult fly usually lays eggs on the fruit in midsummer. After the eggs hatch, the larvae then tunnel into the fruit. To control these insects, do the following:

✓ Rotate crops

✓ Cover youthful plants with row covers

✓ Grow types like 'Serrano' and 'Jalapeño' which are less appealing to the maggots

✓ Hang yellow sticky traps prior to the raised up gently lay eggs. Remove rotten fruits which will harbor the flies until you hang on the traps. Peppers and eggplants normally have fewer insect problems than their own tomato cousins, however they discuss such diseases and pests because blossom fall, sunscald, blossom-end rot, fruit worms (also referred to as corn earworms), and Verticillium wilt. Harvesting tips

Peppers and eggplants are excellent to develop as you don't need to wait till the veggies are fully mature before you select them. Consider your choices for both veggies:

√ Peppers: You're able to select and revel in sweet peppers or wait till they ripen to yellow, orange, or reddish for a sweeter flavor. Spicy peppers change in their hotness based on anxiety. Stressed peppers are somewhat milder, so in the event that you withhold fertilizer and water once the hot peppers have been ripening, you can boost the warmth in the peppers' taste. Cool, cloudy weather will create hot peppers less sexy.

√ Eggplants: You are able to select eggplants in just about any stage. The key is not to let them Become over mature; differently the feel will get soft and mushy. To test Eggplant maturity, see the fruit's skin. A dull-colored skin means it is over mature. Double-check by clipping to the fruit and taking a look at the seeds. Brown-colored seeds are just another indication of over adulthood. An easy test for Maturity will be to push the eggplant's skin with your fingernail. If the skin bounces back, the veggies are ready to harvest. If your nail indents skin, The veggies are over mature. If your veggies are really older and rotting on the Vine, just select them and toss them out; they will not taste really good. The key to Harvesting would be to do it frequently. The More Frequently you crop, the sugars and Eggplants you're getting. To harvest, cut peppers and eggplants using a sharp knife Just over the surface of the green cap onto the fruit. The fruits will last to Ripen once you harvest them so keep them in a cool location. If you would like to dry your peppers, select them when they grow and hang them to dry in a living area with good airflow.

What Are the Mistakes That You Have To Avoid

Knowing the requirements of the plant varieties that you have chosen and providing for them can ensure the healthy growth of your plants. Aside from pests and diseases, lacking in soil nutrients is a common problem that tends to inhibit the growth and maturity of your plants. Potting mixes are actually the best for container gardens to ensure the right amounts of nutrients for the plants. But if this is not enough then occasional application of organic fertilizers become a necessity.

If you can buy some compost (or better produce your own), then apply this on top of the soil and try to dig a bit to mix the compost and aerate the soil. This will loosen up the soil and facilitate the seeping in of nutrients.

You can check on the color of your containers if the plants start to wither despite all the caring and attention that you have provided. Dark-colored containers absorb heat easily, and therefore should be replaced if your plants have been dying and you do not know why. Avoid using dark-colored containers to prevent damage to your plant and wastage of resources.

Keep a listing of suppliers of various material requirements. Try to find out also which agency or authority can be found nearest your area. You can consult and seek expert's advice if you encounter serious problems on your gardening.

What Are Some Common Mistakes I Should Know About?

Face the fact that you are going to make mistakes with container gardening. I've certainly made my share of them so I want to give you some of the most common ones gardeners make so you will know what to expect. Maybe you will do better than I did at my first attempts. Even though I experienced my share of mishaps, I still love container gardening as it is extremely rewarding and can become addictive.

Here is a list to make you more aware and better informed as a gardener as you tend your garden:

1. When dealing with large heavy containers, don't wait to move them at the end of the process ~ Do not make the mistake of filling up a large container with soil and your new plants and then try to move it. Put it where you want it to be and then proceed with filling it with soil and plants.

2. You forget to pay attention to proportions ~ A large container that is filled with stunted and stubby plants is going to look awkward. A good rule to incorporate into your gardening is to try to have at least one plant that will grow a tall as your container is high. Once you have chosen one that will do this, you can plant other vegetation in the same container that is shorter and may even grow down the sides.

3. You drown your plants ~ Make sure your container has plenty of holes in the bottom so when you water, the excess water can drain out. Knowing when to water can be as simple as sticking your finger into the soil to see if it is dry or moist. If it feels dry

to your fingertips, then it is probably time to give your plant a drink.

4. You deprive your plants of water ~ While overwatering your plant is not good, under watering your plant is not any better. Many container gardens need watering at least once a day, especially during the summer time. For hanging plants or plants placed in small containers, they will need watering more than once a day because they have less soil to hold water and moisture. (See, I told you this could be tricky!)

5. You starve your plants ~ Potting mix is the most common ingredient used in container gardens. Unfortunately, these types of mixes don't usually contain enough nutrients for the plants to grow and flourish for the season. To compensate for the few nutrients potting mixes have, you will need to feed them fertilizers. There are many fertilizers to choose from, but the right kind will depend upon your choice of plants.

6. You are too cheap to buy good plants ~ Like everyone, you may be tempted to purchase plants you see in big boxes at cheap prices because you think they will save you money. However, cheap doesn't always mean plants in good condition. Instead, try buying excellent quality plants from reputable stores because they are often healthier plants and have smaller chances to attract diseases and pests. Reputable stores often offer a money back guarantee if the plants prove to be diseased or die.

7. You do not have realistic expectations ~ If you are gone away from home a great deal, you need to consider a self-watering

system or enlist the help of a neighbor or family member. Also, consider your living style and personality.

- If you are low key and casual, you probably should not strive for vegetation that requires a lot of pruning, trimming, and manicuring.

- If you like to live on the wild side of life, then vibrant colors are probably more to your liking than evergreens.

- If cooking everything from scratch is not your style, many homegrown herbs are probably not how you want to fill your containers.

The goal is to experiment and have fun with your garden so that you can enjoy the beauty your garden brings and the fun you have growing your plants.

8. You are afraid to prune your plants ~ It is ironic that some plants do best when we cut off limbs. Tomato plants are like this. If you have too many branches, some of the plant's energy is expended on growing branches rather than producing fruit.

If you notice your plants look like they need a good haircut, get out your pruning shears and cut them off. This is part of the learning process. If your plant ends up looking rough after you get done with it, consider relocating it until you think it looks better; then move it back where you want it to be seen and enjoyed later on—that is, if it ever recovers!

Nurturing Vegetables and Plant Directory

Tomatoes

Tomatoes tend to be one of the vegetables people grow in containers when they first start gardening. Here are a few important things to know about tomatoes:

1. If you decide to grow them, plant them in a large container that is at least fourteen inches in diameter. Additionally, when larger pots are used, tomato plants often respond by getting bigger and producing more fruit.

2. When buying soil for your containers, make sure they are labeled appropriately for larger pots. These will contain ingredients like perlite, composted pine bark, peat moss, rice hulls, coconut pieces, and peanut shells to give your soil some bulk. Avoid mixtures that are high in peat moss because these

will cause compression of your soil, thus causing the plant's root mass to be reduced.

3. You will need a vertical support system, like a small trellis. This should be installed around your tomato plant soon after planting so you do not damage your plant as it grows.

4. Never overwater your tomatoes and be sure to keep the soil moist instead of wet. You cold use self-watering containers to make sure that the plant gets the water it needs.

5. You will want to feed your plants with a slow-release fertilizer and provide it with at least six to eight hours of sunlight every day. It is best to plant tomatoes in the late spring as this lessens their chances of being damaged from frosts.

6. Harvesting tomatoes when they are red means they have reached maturity and are ready to be enjoyed.

Peppers

If you decide to grow peppers, which are also quite popular, strive to find varieties that are labeled, "intended for containers" or "compact." This means these varieties tend not to grow as big as regular varieties meant for in-ground gardens. Here are some helpful facts to know about peppers:

1. Peppers don't require too much space to grow. You can grow them in containers starting at nine inches in diameter and about nine inches deep.

2. You will want to buy soil that is labeled for larger containers because this includes bulk materials like pine bark, peanut shells and other hulls which will help keep the soil from becoming too dense. Also, make sure the soil remains moist, even when its surface becomes dried out.

3. Be sure to supply trellis support for your peppers so when they become tall, they will not become damaged by falling over.

4. You can feed it with fertilizer once every week and cover the soil with mulch so it will retain moisture.

5. Sunlight exposure should be direct in the morning and filtered all day long as the afternoon sun can actually burn the crop.

6. Peppers are usually grown during early spring.

7. The peppers are ready to pick when their color and size have reached maturity.

Beans

Beans are another vegetable easily grown in containers. Beans are tasty, easy to grow, and they freeze well, too. Here are a few recommendations if you decide to grow your own:

1. You will need a container about twelve inches wide. If you are growing bush beans, the container depth should be six to seven inches, whereas pole beans require a depth closer to eight or nine inches.

2. With several varieties, you will need to provide a trellis for the plant to grow up on to support the weight of the plant.

3. Consider using pasteurized soil (soil that has been baked in the oven), mix it with compost, and add mulch to help retain the soil's moisture.

4. Make sure you place your containers in a warm or brightly lit location but avoid direct sunlight.

5. You may need to water the beans frequently to keep the soil moist, too.

6. You can plant your seedlings in the spring once the soil has warmed up.

7. When the pods are fully elongated and are crisp and firm, it is time to harvest them. When they reach maturity, be sure to harvest them every day. Frequent harvesting will encourage more beans to be produced from your plant.

Squash/Zucchini

Squash and zucchini fall into the cucurbit category of plants (as do cucumbers). These may not be vegetables you think of right away for growing, but they are not difficult to do and are delicious straight from the garden—raw or cooked. Here are several guidelines to be aware of:

1. Cucurbit plants can be grown in any container that is twelve inches in diameter. Two plants are easily grown side by side in a fourteen-inch-diameter container.

2. Choose a good quality potting soil and mix it with organic matter before planting your seedlings.

3. Make sure your plants get at least eight hours of sunlight per day and be sure to water them often. Do more watering if your container is made of clay rather than plastic because this type of container can cause the soil to dry out faster.

4. Begin to fertilize your plants with a timed-release formula after the first real leaves begin to appear.

5. Plant your seedlings in early to mid-summer. This variety of plants are actually very easy to start from seeds, taking about three to four weeks before it is time to transplant into containers. However, many like me just plant the seeds directly into the containers.

6. Depending upon the varieties you choose, cucurbits begin to ripen after 45 days. Consider starting new plants four to six weeks after your initial planting to keep produce fresh throughout the summer.

7. Winter squashes will be ready to harvest about 100 days after planting. If you planted summer squashes, you can pick them when the fruits become about eight inches long and three inches in diameter.

Cucumbers

Because cucumbers are in the cucurbit family, much of what I stated above applies here as well.

1. You need to use a large container that has a diameter of at least 12 inches.

2. Cucumbers need loose soil that reaches 70 degrees Fahrenheit and has good drainage.

3. They also need organic fertilizer to sustain their nutritional needs.

4. Cucumbers are plants that need eight hours of direct exposure to sunlight.

5. Harvest your cucumbers when they are about seven to nine inches long.

Lettuces

Lettuces fall into four different categories: Loose Leaf, Romaine (also known as Cos), Butterheads, and Crisphead. While each has their own characteristics, there are some similarities between them:

1. It is best to plant lettuce seeds directly into a six- to twelve-inch-diameter container that you want them to grow in. They do not transplant well. They only take about one week to germinate and make sure your plants are eight to ten inches apart.

2. Lettuces tend to grow best in cooler temperatures.

3. Use a standard soil mix formulated to provide nutrients and one that will hold moisture. You can mix the soil with compost to make it even healthier.

4. These vegetables grow very successfully in containers, enabling you to keep pests, snails and slugs under control.

5. Do not place these vegetables in direct sunlight. Instead, place them in a shady place for best results.

6. Lettuces need to be harvested within a week of when they are ready or the leaves will begin to bolt. When this happens, a flower stalk will appear, will go to seed, and the leaves become bitter tasting. Therefore, plant only the amount you plan to use.

7. The plant itself grows quickly, especially when soil conditions are healthy.

8. Be sure your containers drain well but also make sure the soil remains moist.

9. Lettuce plants require little to no fertilizer, if you are using good soil.

10. Lettuces will be ready to harvest anywhere from eight to fourteen weeks.

11. The best method for enjoying lettuce throughout the growing season is to plan to sow a few lettuce seeds every two weeks. Then, when you harvest the lettuce, be sure to put up the whole plant. This will discourage diseases in the ground and rotting.

Potatoes

Potatoes come in so many beautiful colors like blue, yellow, purple, and read as well as various shapes. Growing potatoes in containers is slightly different from other vegetables but they can grow quite successfully. In fact, growing them in containers actually minimizes problems with contaminates in the soil and susceptibility to pests. Here are some overall guidelines:

1. Use a deep container to grow your potatoes in because they need depth in order to mature. Consider using one that is fourteen to sixteen inches deep and has good drainage.

2. While potatoes are available at many gardening and nursery centers, it is also possible to grow potatoes using potatoes bought from the grocery store. However, make sure they are organically grown because some potatoes have been chemically treated so they won't produce "eyes"—a necessary element for growing them. In addition, consider ones that have signs of sprouting.

3. For the soil, use potting soil with multipurpose compost and an organic fertilizer.

4. Potato pieces with eyes are placed on top of a few inches of soil, then covered with about six inches of soil. As the plant grows upward, additional soil is added—about a shovel full every two weeks.

5. These plants need moist soil, so be sure the soil does not dry out.

6. Place the potatoes in an area where it is partially shaded and partially exposed to sunlight. They require about six to eight hours of sunlight each day. Direct sunlight for long periods of the day is not good for these plants.

Eggplant

Eggplant is a vegetable that grows very well, especially if you purchase ones that are labeled "compact" for containers. There are several other guidelines you will want to know about before growing these:

1. Each plant needs to be planted in containers twelve to fourteen inches in diameter to thrive and up to three plants can be planted in the same container if you use a pot that is at least twenty inches in diameter.

2. Use a mixture of potting soil and sand to ensure that the plant gets the nutrients and moisture it needs.

3. You should plan to feed your plant on a weekly basis with a soluble fertilizer.

4. Some varieties will need a short support system. Two to three ringed supports used for tomatoes work well. Be sure to install them right after planting so you don't damage your plant trying to put them in after the plant has grown significantly.

5. Make sure to allow your plant to get eight hours of direct sunlight and keep the soil moist at all times.

6. For most temporal climates, eggplant should not be planted until early April because these plants need a warmer growing environment.

How Do I Prepare For Winter and Provide Good Growing Conditions

Wintertime comes around every year and there are certain things you will want to think about in order to prepare your plants and containers for the cold weather.

1. Start with your containers

Glazed pots and terracotta clay pots are quite porous and can easily crack in freezing temperatures. Be sure to empty these containers, place them in a sheltered area, and position them upside down. Cover them with plastic to add extra protection to prolong the life of your containers.

2. Stop fertilizing plants during midsummer

This is one of the best ways to prepare your plants for freezing temperatures. Terminating fertilizers will reduce new growth on your plants, keeping them from being so vulnerable to frost. This is especially appropriate in plants that normally slow down their growth or become dormant when temperatures drop.

3. Consider your space and light sources

There are plants such as peppers and tomatoes that have the capacity to produce fruit even during the winter. If these plants are provided with enough light and are placed in containers that are large enough, they can be brought indoors.

4. Place potted plants into a larger container

To help plants thrive and survive cooler temperatures, place your potted plants inside larger containers. Once you do so, fill in the sides between the outside of the smaller pot and the inside of the larger pot with additional soil or mulch. This will insulate the plant's roots from the cold temperatures.

5. Bury your container in the ground

One of the things you can do to protect your plant for the winter is to bury your container in the ground. Make sure the top part of the container is on the same level with the top of the ground. If there is less soil in the container, fill it so the soil is level with the ground. Water could accumulate and freeze inside the container if it's not filled with soil.

6. Cover your plants with a generous amount of mulch

Cover the surface of your containers with mulch, especially when the soil is close to freezing. The mulch should be about two to four inches thick. Check your plant regularly and be sure to add additional mulch if necessary.

Plants will grow happily in containers as long as they are provided with enough water, food and light. Choosing the plants and crops to grow should be straightforward and as containers give you more control over the localized environment in which the plants grow you may be able to grow a wider variety of plants than would be the case if you were simply growing direct in the ground.

The environment that you create for your plants will have an impact on what you can grow but the amount of light available will be significant in terms of choice. Consider the most suitable plants for the conditions when you first establish your container garden – with experience you may wish to experiment with various techniques.

Leafy plants will need a minimum of six hours of sunshine and fruit bearing plants will require around eight hours per day. Many tomato varieties will require up to ten hours, while root crops may require much less. Even with more control over your plant's environment the amount of available sun should be taken into consideration when choosing varieties.

How to Create Containers for Different seasons

If you believe that building a successful container garden is a humongous task, here is a reality check for you. It is a sequential three-step process, which includes buying a suitable container, preparing it for planting and installing the plant into the container. It truly is just as simple as it sounds. However, one significant difference between container gardening and soil gardening is that former requires more care and attention as compared to the latter. You have to pay much more attention to the soil mix that you are using, watering schedule and fertilization. Besides, location of the plant and plant chosen also play a significant role in the success or failure of the container garden.

The first step towards preparing the container for planting is to fill the container with an appropriate soil mix. You can choose the soil mix that is best suited for the plant that you are planning to grow in this container. However, as a general rule, the soil mix should have a good drainage system and must be able to hold enough water required, by any plant, to sustain. You can find several varieties of these at any garden center, and if you are unable to make a choice, you can always seek help of the retailer to decide which soil mix is right for your plant-container combination.

A word of advice for you is that you must moisten the bagged soil mix before using. This makes the process of preparing the container easier. You must fill the container to the top leaving about one inch space from the top edge. This is done to ensure that some space is left, on the top of the container, to accommodate for the water that you will put in the container. Before the water is absorbed, the water will stand, and this head space performs this function.

The second most important factor that decides the kind of preparation that the container requires is the type of plant you are planning to grow. However, how these plants are arrangements in the container depends on the location of the container. For instance, if you plan to keep the container at a place that can be viewed from all sides, you must plant the tall plant at the center and short ones on the circumference. On the other hand, if the planter is to be placed against the wall and can be viewed only from the front, the tall plant can be planted at the back, and small plants can cover the front circumference of the container.

If you are a beginner and not sure which arrangement will look best, you can simply put the plants on the top layer of the soil to get a better idea of what the final arrangement will look like. In this way, you can make the required adjustments, and once the design is finalized, you can go ahead with the planting. If you are replanting the plant, look at the roots closely, to ensure that they are not coiled and then plant them in the pot at the same level as they were planted in the original container.

Another facet of the process of planting in a container is to decide the number of plants that you want in a single container. This maximum number of plants that you can plant in a container depends on the capacity of the container. You can choose to plant any number of plants less than this. You can also leave spaces between plants and add plants later on if budget is an issue.

Once the planting is done, ensure that you water the container thoroughly. This is particularly crucial as the first time you water the container, the water must be enough to eliminate the air pockets that may exist near the root balls of the plant. So, how would you know that the plant has got its water? Water the plant until water begins to come out of the drainage hole. In addition, perform this activity several times for best results.

The biggest advantage of container gardening is that it allows you to enjoy the pleasure of gardening throughout the year. As seasons change, you change the plants in your containers to ensure that the lively look of the place remains alive all through the year. This is how container gardening performs the dual functionality of helping you explore your gardening side and brushing your creative skills to create beautiful arrangements that are capable of becoming the focal points of your house.

The number of times you change the plants of your containers mainly depends on the money and time that you are ready to invest in container gardening. While you can change all the plants every season, you can also consider changing only a few plants to add a refreshing look to the existing arrangement.

How to Choose Your Container

There are various containers that come in different sizes and shapes which can be used for container gardening. These containers may be made out of clay, plastic, polyethylene, metal and glass. If you wish to recycle, you can also use old milk jugs, barrels, boxes, baskets and even ice cream containers. Basically, you can choose to use whichever container you want. However, you need to take into consideration the amount of size and space your plants need to grow in, how deep their roots grow, as well as whether or not the containers will allow good drainage and aeration.

Materials of Containers

The material of the container you choose to grow your plants in is very important. The container materials can be categorized into two: porous and non-porous.

- Porous. Porous materials are usually made out of clay or terracotta. They come in a wide range of sizes and shapes and are easily available at many garden stores. These pots are good for drainage and ventilation, but you will need to monitor your plants more often for watering, as water is absorbed much faster. Clay or terracotta pots can be a good material to use if you are looking for a classic design. However, if you plan to grow heavy plants and move your plants around, you might want to choose a different container material, as these containers are easily breakable.

- Non-porous. Non-porous container materials can be made out of plastic, metal or glass. If you want a light container so you can easily move it around, you can choose to use plastic. Not only is it easily moveable, but it is also very cheap. This can be an ideal material to use, especially if you plan to take care of numerous plants. You can also use glass so you can see the growth of the roots. Glass containers can be great decorations, especially if your plants are colorful.

Container gardens look their best when there is a sense of balance between the containers and the plants. Make sure that each plant is correctly fitted to a container so they can grow to their maximum potential. Besides, it is never a good idea to transfer plants once they have grown, as it will stress them out and eventually cause them to wilt.

Picking the Right Containers

In truth, there is no specific or right container to use for container gardening. There are so many containers that you can choose to use. You can decide to use pots, old jugs or cartons or even watering cans. But to help you choose among hundreds of choices, here are some guidelines that you can follow.

- Style of the container. There are hundreds or even thousands of container styles. You can choose to use anything that you want at all. You can grow your plant in a clay pot, a fish bowl, in a shoe box or even in a trash can. Your choice will mainly depend on your budget, your design preference and the type of plant that you wish to grow.

- Size of the container. Of course, the larger the container, the higher the chance that your plants will grow healthy and strong. The advantage of using larger pots is that you need to water less frequently because the more soil there is, the longer the moisture will be held. However, if your space is limited, then you need to consider planting smaller plants that can survive in a limited space.

- Self-watering container. If you frequently travel or want a container garden but do not have that much time to tend to it, you can purchase a self-watering container to make sure that your plants get watered regularly. A self-watering container is very convenient to own, but if you live in an area where it mostly rains, you might have to monitor your plants more closely to make sure that they do not drown and die.

- Drainage. As mentioned earlier, you can choose to use any container that you want but you have to make sure that it has holes for drainage or it is a material that you can easily make holes in.

Types of Containers

It is a good idea to put some thought into what type containers you want to use. If you are on a tight budget, you might be tempted to go with the cheapest you are able to locate at your neighborhood retail center. While these will still work, they are not the ideal choice.

By far, the most popular choice for containers is plastic. They're inexpensive, lightweight, durable and fashionable since they come in a wide array of colors and styles.

Some people choose more porous materials for their containers. The good news is that their porosity allows air to enter and exit the root system, giving a higher percentage of oxygen than standard containers. The bad news is that this air movement also means that the dirt dries out faster, requiring more diligent watering.

Then there is the old reliable choice: clay pots. Many find these appealing because they are relatively lightweight for their size and they can withstand a lot of use. They also allow the artist in you to paint them to match your style, if you so desire. They even come with a drain hole built right in. Their only down side is they are not meant for the cold. If moisture is left in them, even wet dirt, the expansion from the low temperatures will crack them.

But there are some things to watch out for. While the list of features given above can sound rather appealing, it can also be your undoing.

Price. There is inexpensive and then there is cheap. The difference might not be substantial considering the fact that we're talking about plastic, but the end result can be huge. Inexpensive means that it fits your budget. Cheap means it won't last and you'll end up replacing it too early, thus negating the original savings that you pocketed. Don't always go with the lowest price; also consider quality and durability.

Durability. This goes right along with price as you get what you pay for. It might be lightweight, but it also has to last and handle the load of the plant. If you have to move a container and it buckles from the load, you risk losing your plant.

Something else to consider is that you might have to move the container at some point. So make sure that what you pick is durable enough to withstand the move. Even if it manages being moved, it also needs to be easy to hold onto. A flimsy container that easily buckles might not crack or break when picked up, but its shape can be distorted from the weight, making it rather difficult to juggle until you can get it to its new location.

Your containers need to be able to handle what the weather can dish out—especially a blazing sun for long periods of time. Cheap, lightweight plastic containers will crack after just a short amount of exposure to the blistering sun. Once a small crack forms, it won't take long for it to devour the container.

If you are sold on using plastic, the best advice would be to go with plastic containers that are double-walled. This provides more protection and durability for the money. Plus, the additional layer of plastic walling allows the heat from the sun to dissipate more instead of heating up the dirt surrounding your plant. This means your plant has less of a chance of drying out before you water it again.

Drainage. Some plastic containers are manufactured without a drainage hole. This leaves the responsibility of providing one for your plants up to you. In order to do this, you will need to utilize a power drill and drill a reasonably sized hole in the middle of the bottom of the container.

Some people prefer to drill numerous smaller holes instead of one large hole. While this is fine, it can produce more drainage than you anticipate. Once the holes are there, you are committed to using them. Keeping one large hole is easier to manage in the event that the loss of water needs to be better controlled.

If the container is quite large, it may be necessary to drill several large holes to adequately drain the plant considering the increased surface area.

If you purchase containers that have pre-drilled drainage holes in them, there will be times when these holes are too large, allowing not only too much water to escape but also dirt, as well. The best way to remedy this is to use a drainage screen.

Drainage screens are pieces of mesh that more than cover the diameter of the drainage hole, while still allowing excess moisture to be released. Drainage screens can be purchased pre-cut or you can buy a section of the screening and custom make your own pieces. The screening is inexpensive and saves you a lot of heartache from lost soil. If you can't find drainage screening in your local store or if you don't have the opportunity to shop for it, then a piece of an old window screen will work nicely.

Pre-owned. It is also common for new gardeners to pick up used pots from a number of sources, such as friends, family, other gardeners, yard sales, etc. These are still fine to use as long as you exercise a little caution. Make sure to thoroughly clean all containers with warm soapy water before use as they could be harboring some unpleasantness that you won't want to bring into your container garden.

Since you don't know the history behind the container or what was placed in it, it is better to be safe than sorry. Old dirt can contain everything from pesticides to old salt deposits, mold, disease, weeds and even the eggs of insects. Scrub your containers with a plastic brush to make sure everything has been cleaned before using. Simply rinsing it out with water will not do the trick.

Tips for Container Plants

We have offered adequate pointers on choosing the right container, space, location and other essential requirements that mark the success of container gardening. The focus will be on suitable planting and caring measures that one needs to keep in mind for increased success of their container garden or landscape. Read on for more information!

Easy Steps to Plant in Containers

☐ Choose a container and begin by closing the drainage spots that is if they are too big. They should be just enough to allow the excess water to drain out but not the soil along with it. Fill about two thirds of the pot with potting mix.

☐ Allow the plants to sit in the container and decide on your arrangement. You can either have the tallest plants placed in the center and the smaller ones around them or vice versa, which ever best appeals to your arrangement style.

☐ Gently remove the plants from the soil, taking care not to be too harsh or destructive to the roots or stems of the plant. Place it gently on the chosen container and insert it into the soil, following the same measurements of depth as the pot you extracted it from.

☐ Add extra soil to the plants, especially in between and use your hands gently but firmly to place it. Take care not to be too hard as that will damage the plant and cause breakage.

☐ Move your pot to its perfect spot where it is greeted by a daily dose of healthy sunlight.

☐ Water it regularly and add fertilizers as per schedule and enjoy the efforts of your hard work.

Easy Steps for Maintaining Containers

☐ Depending on your climatic condition, you can plan a watering schedule. Ideally watering your container once in every 2 days is sufficient but in areas that are too hot and humid, watering every day is a must for healthy plant growth.

☐ For added nutrition, feed your plants with bloom boosting or all-purpose plant food once in about 2 weeks or as per the instructions given on the plant food cover.

☐ Take care to adopt deadheading which is a process of removing all the used blooms which further encourages the growth of new blooms. Take care not to just pull off the dead leaves, instead study them carefully and remove gently if required.

☐ Every once in a while, gently tap or pinch the stem of your plants as this will encourage stimulation which further encourages the growth of new branches and stems.

Grooming with your container garden

The main aim or the purpose of maintaining a container garden is its aesthetic appeal. Thus, it is very essential to groom the container garden, every now and then. The basic groom would include the general cleaning, pinching and deadhead removal.

The general cleaning includes removing dead and dried leaves, applying medicines for keeping away insects and diseases, soil plowing and sprinkling water on the leaves, to rid the plant off dust. The pinching refers to removal of the growing node in the plant. This will reduce the height of the plant and increase the width of the plant and would give it a bushy appearance. The deadhead removal is very essential in flowering plants. After the flower is bloomed and dried, the head of the stem would be retained. This would prevent the new leaves from growing. Thus, it is essential to remove these deadheads.

Color for grooming

Nothing can groom your garden more than colors. You need to pick the right colored plants and the right container. If you plant a pink flowering plant in a violet container on a yellow wall as a decoration, you would end up having a cluster of colors in your living room. If you happen to have a violet container, use violet, white, blue, or cream color flowering plants. Place it along with the things which are in shades of violet, blue and lavender. This would give you, a color shade to work on.

Use small vines that would fall from the edges of the pot. This might help in concealing the color of the container and give a green bunch-like appearance. Buying small paint cans to paint the container as per requirement can also be done. There are a lot of ways to play with colors, when it comes to container gardening. You can create a method, look for the flaws and try again and again. It is almost impossible to get it right, in the first attempt. People There are a lot of online galleries to give you an idea to use the colors, in the right way.

Container placement

There are three main ways to place containers. The first one is linear way. You can keep it in a straight line along the window still, wherever possible. The second method is to place it in definite shapes. If you have a very large living room, in the middle of the room, arrange all the containers in a circular shape or in square or triangular shapes. The last method is hanging. Use spillers to give a more appealing look to your hanging baskets.

Placing one container is not a big deal. You can place it anywhere, in any angle and direction. When it comes to containers with different heights, shapes and colors, you would need to make sure that combining the containers should not spoil the overall display. There is rule as to how you can place the containers. You can place them according to the look of your house or the utility of the room.

Grooming with other materials

You can use other materials for grooming your containers. You can use any material of your choice. Here are a few tips to groom your garden with different materials.

a)

Make a small fountain and cover it with an open bottom container. It would look like a fountain and also as a bird bath.

b)

Use pebbles to cover the surface of the containers. Use pebbles of colors which would match the flower or simply, cream colored pebbles.

c)

Use a large aquarium. Place many containers of aquatic plants in it and also surround the aquarium with small containers.

d)

For vines and climbers, build a steel ornamental rod in the middle of four or five containers with climbers of different colors and textures. Let the climbers cover the rod.

Water container garden

Buy a transparent container and plant aquatic plants in it. Snails can be added to the containers to control the growth of algae. If you grow a lot of water container plants, make sure to take precautions to avoid mosquito breeding as well as frog breeding. The water should be free from chlorine, if you want fish to thrive. You should ideally keep one fish for every 5 gallons of water.

Grooming tips and basic ideas

There are a lot of ways to improve the décor of the house, with the help of containers. Here are a few tips which would help you to do so.

a) In a large shallow container, place violas and blue Phlox. Use concrete containers and plant them near your pond.
b) If your walls are yellow or brown in color, use pansies, violas, grass, Ivy and Panolas in brown large containers.
c) If you have a kennel, use magnolia, spider plant and caladium to hide the downspouts. This combination would suit all wall colors.
d) Agave with pebbles would be suitable for wooden floors and pool side decorations.
e) When it comes to succulents, you can add a lot of different types in one container and use it as the centerpiece, while decorating with your containers.
f) If you want to create simple containers, use caladiums and grasses. This would not add much to the décor but, would help to fill places without disturbing the décor.
g) If you want to add useful vegetation to the ornamental containers, lettuce would be a very good choice. Lettuce with geranium and marigold is a good choice.
h) If you want to add height to the container, use rosemary.
i) If you want a plant to twine around the fence or grills, use Mandeville.

These are a few tips which would help to add beauty to your house. Everything from hanging ferns to basic grass can be used to increase the aesthetic appeal of the containers. The other combinations that would work are;

a) Lettuce, violas and mums

b) Elephant ear and sweet potato vine

c) Boxwood and violas

d) Purple fountain grass, Begonias and coleus

e) Coleus and lantana

f) Agave, Japanese rood iris and lavender

g) Mixed greens with white impatiens

h) Chives garden, parsley and cilantro

i) Violas, pansies and daffodils

j) Impatiens and dwarf spruce

k) Dichondra and Begonia

l) Ferns, ivy, begonia, impatiens and spider plant

m) Thyme garden, rosemary and coriander

n) Peppers, crotons and marigold

o) Multicolored violas

p) Grape hyacinth and daffodils

q) Silver foliage and white flowers

r) Grasses, foxgloves, tulips and pansies

s) Petunia, cypress and begonias

Managing Pests and Diseases

Pest management is a very important part of any type of gardening – especially container gardening because your pots and planters are usually close to your home or inside, and you don't want to have to deal with insects in your living area. Traditional pest management utilizes chemical treatments to either deal with an infestation or avoid one. However, scientific research has discovered (and continues to discover) just how harmful those chemicals can be to the environment as well your own personal health. In this guide, chemicals will not be suggested, recommended, or encouraged because they are so detrimental to many areas of life. Instead, you will soon learn that there are many organic alternatives that can help you grow the container garden you want to without exposing you or the planet to harmful toxins while doing so.

Pest management is a battle on two fronts – prevention and treatment.

Preventing Pests from Damaging Your Container Garden

Remember the age-old proverb, "A pound of prevention is worth a ton of cure"? This rings especially true when it comes to gardening. Of course preventing an insect infestation is beneficial in and of itself, but that prevention also protects a potential food source (i.e. your growing vegetables) making it doubly important. It is much easier and less time consuming if you can stop those destructive insects before they even become a noticeable issue.

Some great pest prevention tips to consider implementing include:

Plant Choices – Some plants are more resistant to pests than others are, and that is usually indicated on the packaging of the seeds themselves. Look for labeling that says something about being resistant to specific pests and diseases. When you see such labeling, it has two possible meanings. Either those seeds are engineered in a way to be less attractive to insects compared to other seeds of the same type, or the plants are naturally designed to withstand a significant amount of damage from pests without affecting the produce being grown. Whichever characteristic is true for seeds labeled as pest-resistant, the final outcome is an eventual harvest that needs much less intervention for pest control than what might normally occur.

Companion Planting – Even better than pest-resistant seeds is the implementation of companion gardening. Companion gardening is when specific plants are grown close to other plants that are known to provide a natural resistance to pests that would otherwise threaten the viability of the central plant. For example, potato plants and marigold flowers repel the Mexican bean beetles that can destroy bush bean plants. Growing borage by strawberries, tomatoes, and squash makes them unattractive to tomato worms. Moths that are bent on devouring cabbages can be avoided by planting marigolds nearby them as well. Celery plants will repel some kinds of cabbageworms, and onions can repel flies that target carrots. Growing corn fights Japanese beetles and aphids that often attack carrots, apples, berries, tomatoes, and more. Did you decide on growing those cucumbers for your family's insatiable desire for pickles? Make sure to plant radishes in a container nearby because the radishes will repel cucumber beetles.

There are many plant configurations that can benefit your container gardening efforts, and many of them depend on your own particular goals and the plants you're. The use of companion planting is one of the best organic gardening tips you can utilize in order to grow healthy vegetables safely without the use of chemical pesticides.

General Repellents, Deterrents, and Treatments

Nature has been designed with such unbelievable and intricate complexity that mankind has yet to discover all the ways the planet can protect itself quite naturally with healthy techniques that are good for plant, human, and environmental safety. We don't need chemical repellants and deterrents to keep pests and diseases away from our plants…God has provided many natural options to use as needed that aren't destructive to the planet like most man-made chemicals are.

Coffee Grounds – Would you believe that used coffee grounds can be one of your greatest weapons against a variety of pests that might seek to destroy your plants? Sprinkle old coffee grounds around any plants that are dealing with slugs and snails attacking them. Coffee grounds will also help keep cats and squirrels out of your containers while providing a plant-enriching boost of nitrogen at the same time.

Flowers – Many flowers and herbs do double duty as pest repellents. Marigolds and lavender are both great options if you struggle with mosquito control in your area since mosquitoes do not care for the fragrances released by those particular flowers.

Diatomaceous Earth – DE just might become your favorite gardening aid when it comes to keeping your container plants healthy and happy. If you don't know what diatomaceous earth (a.k.a. DE) is, it is a powdery natural substance comprised of the dried remains of algae. Food-grade DE is 100% natural and safe for humans, plants, and animals, but no so safe for destructive bugs – especially those known to damage fragile plants. It is surprisingly inexpensive which is just another aspect that makes it a gardener's favorite. DE can be sprinkled on the soil around the plant, and it should be used to dust the plant itself as frequently as needed. The one negative aspect of DE is the benefits greatly decrease once it gets wet. If your plants are outside and exposed to rainy weather, just plan on reapplying the earth when the rain stops. It's great if your plants are indoors because you won't need to keep re-dusting your plants with DE every time it gets washed off in the rain.

 Plant Collars – A plant collar is exactly what it sounds like...a collar that goes around the circumference of a plant to protect it from crawling and extremely destructive pests like cutworms. Collars can be made of just about anything you might have hanging around or that you might find in a recycling bin somewhere. You can fashion collars out of plastic, cardboard, tin, etc. Collars need to be pushed into the soil around your plant about an inch deep, and they should have at least three inches of collar above the soil in order to provide the needed protection.

Baking Soda – Baking soda isn't just for the kitchen any more. It has many other uses outside of baking, etc., and one of those uses is in your garden. Worried about fungus on your plants? Make an organic fungicide by mixing four teaspoons of baking soda with one gallon of water. Spray your plants with this mixture as soon as new little produce becomes visible on your plants. If cabbageworms are a problem, mix equal parts of baking soda and flour then dust affected plants with the mixture, and your problem with the plant-destroying creatures will soon be a distant memory. (A bonus benefit of baking soda is it makes a great hand scrub after you've been in the nitty-gritty soil of container gardening. Keep a cup of it by your sink, and your dirty hands will clean up easily.)

Conclusion

I hope throughout the course, you have become excited about the unlimited possibilities of vegetable container gardening. Here is an edible hobby and pastime that offers you creativity for your expressions as well as food for your table.

Although this guide is designed for beginning gardeners starting their adventure into the land of vegetable container gardening, all of the information you just read is beneficial to any gardener regardless of age or experience. Now you know just how simple it can be to grow your own edibles in the middle of city living – even if you have no yard or traditional gardening space.

Container planting is going to have a series of ups and downs associated with it. You need to ensure that you keep pushing forward and learning from your mistakes. That way, you end up expanding your knowledge and improving the overall results that you have in the garden. Remember, even experts had to start with very little knowledge in the garden.

There are many secrets to successful container gardening that the novice gardener may want to keep in mind. This form of gardening is very different from traditional gardening, especially since you must supply soil and nutrients on a routine basis for the plant. Even watering is a little more complex, because there is no room for runoff, rather it soaks through and this causes the ground to remain moist at all times.

With these tips, you should find that you are going to be better off in the garden. It is important to keep in mind that for many of these tips, it will help you to plan things out and to consider the layout of your garden in advance.

Perhaps most importantly, it will be important that you do not give up on your first try. While these tips can increase your chances of success in the garden, it does not mean you will have instant success overnight. However, if you keep each tip in mind and use them to help improve the results that you have, in time you should find that you do end up with a beautiful vegetable garden that you can be proud of.

Within you is the ability to successfully grow a thriving gardener. Make sure you take the time to nurture that individual and do all you can to grow vegetables that you love, within containers that you have around your home. With a little fertilizer, quality soil and the right pots as mentioned in these tips, you are going to end up with a garden that you will love and it will be one that all of your friends talk about for years to come.

Most of all, I hope you have come to understand that you can grow vegetables in containers almost anywhere. Whether you live in a neighborhood where the yards are small or live in a high-rise apartment complex with no yard at all, vegetable container gardening offers opportunities to enjoy bountiful produce. It all comes down to knowing about containers, plants, soils, and techniques.

So, what are you waiting for? Exciting results are waiting for you in the world of vegetable container gardening. And the best part of all is that you can begin most any time of the year.

CPSIA information can be obtained
at www.ICGtesting.com
Printed in the USA
BVHW061912250321
603415BV00014B/1901